——— Stuff Every ———

MOM

Should Know

Copyright © 2012 by Quirk Productions, Inc.

All rights reserved. No part of this book may be reproduced in any form without written permission from the publisher.

Library of Congress Cataloging in Publication Number: 2011933441

ISBN: 978-1-59474-552-2

Printed in the United States of America

Typeset in Goudy and Monotype Old Style

Designed by Katie Hatz
Illustrations by Kate Francis
Production management by John J. McGurk

Quirk Books
215 Church Street
Philadelphia, PA 19106
quirkbooks.com

10 9 8 7 6 5 4 3

Stuff Every Lawyer Should Know: The publisher and author hereby disclaim any liability from any injury that may result from the use, proper or improper, of the information contained in this book. We do not guarantee that this information is safe, complete, or wholly accurate, nor should it be considered a substitute for the reader's good judgment and common sense. In other words: Exercise caution when fielding unsolicited parenting advice. Be über-prepared when taking your baby onboard an airplane (see page 26). And never ever forget the value of an occasional mom's night out.

——— Stuff Every ———

MOM

Should Know

By Heather Gibbs Flett and Whitney Moss

QUIRK BOOKS
PHILADELPHIA

To our moms, step-moms, grandmas,
and husbands

Introduction

Motherhood. We're in it together, aren't we? We firmly believe that this is not a competition between breast feeders vs. bottle feeders or cloth diapers vs. disposables, but rather a community—a secret club that any woman can join. In this book, we'll tell you what we know and what we've learned from other moms. We hope you'll take away what works for you and then share that wisdom with a few other newbies.

Every parenting manual addresses the care and feeding of children, but too few help you with the day-to-day stuff: how to make Mickey Mouse pancakes, what to do with your child's Social Security card, or which household items can be used as toys in a pinch. And that is the real stuff every mom needs to know.

This book arms you with step-by-step instructions to help navigate the tricky scenarios that moms encounter most frequently. We start with babies in their adorable clueless first year and move through the tween years, when you can hardly believe they ever used to fit in your cradled arms. We offer the tips, tricks, and wisdom that come from trial and error—and asking your mom friends for advice.

A lifetime of joy awaits. Also waiting: a lifetime of stuff that needs doing. Being a mom can be messy, funny, and confusing. Fortunately, what you're holding is *Stuff Every Mom Should Know*.

Baby Stuff

Five Fun Things to Do with a Baby

Going on daily outings will help you get comfortable with skills like changing a diaper in public, feeding your baby away from your house, and using a car seat and other gear. Babies don't care where they go, and that's why you should do what you want to do. Get out of the house and introduce your little cutie to the world!

Here are five easy things to do with your baby in tow:

1. **Meet a friend at a café.** Park your stroller next to you and order a hot chocolate. Before you leave, purchase some pastries for that night's dessert.

2. **Go window shopping.** Head for a favorite neighborhood and experiment with using a stroller or soft carrier. If you see a children's shop, go in and ask whether they have a changing table or nursing chair. That way, you'll know where one is when you need it.

3. **See a movie in the theater.** The first showing of the day is typically pretty empty, and some cities even offer special screenings just for moms and babies. Be prepared to feed your baby to keep her occupied—and also to step outside should she fuss loudly enough to disturb other patrons.

4. **Visit your partner at work.** You'll get a lunch date out of it, and your partner will get a chance to show off his new bundle of joy.

5. **Take in a museum exhibition.** It doesn't matter if it's art, science, or automotive history; your baby just wants to be with you, wherever you go.

How to Swaddle a Baby

Swaddling is like origami with your baby. The goal is to wrap her up in surroundings so snug and womblike that she can't wake herself up with flailing arms and legs. Yes, she will fight it. But, ultimately, she probably will love it. And when she sleeps, you can sleep.

1. Take a perfectly square blanket (at least 40 inches on each side) and lay it flat.

2. Fold down corner A at the top so that the new edge is a little wider than her shoulders.

3. Lay her on the blanket with her neck at the crease, her head poking out, and her shoulders on the blanket.

4. Place her right arm comfortably flat against her body. Secure her right arm by tightly wrapping corner B and tucking it under her left armpit, with the excess fabric secured underneath her body.

5. Bring corner C upward over her feet.

6. Take corner D of the blanket and bring it across your baby's chest. Ensure that her

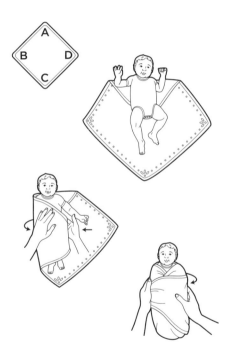

Swaddling is like baby origami.

arm is secure under the fabric. Tuck the excess fabric underneath her.

Voilà. You have made a burrito baby. Use this tecnhique at naptime, bedtime, or whenever you want a non-flailing infant to snuggle. **Note:** Swaddling is not recommended for use in car seats or for babies advanced enough to roll over.

How to Feed a Baby

Until your baby turns one year old, baby milk (either breast milk or formula) will be his primary source of nutrition and calories. But an all-liquid diet can't last forever.

- **When to start?** Your pediatrician will have specific guidelines about the when and the what, but here is our mom-to-mom guideline on starting real food: when your baby can sit up independently and starts grabbing for your spoon when you eat, it's probably time to think about introducing solid foods.

- **Yes, runny is considered solid.** The funny thing is that "solid food" is not very solid at all. At best, it's a thin runny porridge. Babies need practice and exposure to turn their palates on to more tastes and textures. The important thing to remember is to keep this experience positive. Follow his lead on quantity and stop when he seems to have eaten enough. Your first spoon-feeding sessions may last only a few minutes. These experiments are as much about learning to move food from the spoon to the back of his mouth as they are about the new textures.

- **First foods.** One very basic first food is iron-fortified rice cereal. Add breast milk or warmed formula to the cereal, in the ratio of 1 tablespoon of cereal powder for every 4 tablespoons of baby milk. Offer your infant small serving sizes—even just 1 to 2 small spoonfuls. Remember, learning to eat takes practice.

- **Increasing your child's diet.** Introduce other solid foods gradually, spaced out by a few days or a week. Make sure your baby is having no adverse or allergic reaction to one food before introducing another. Contact your doctor if diarrhea, vomiting, or rash develops in response to particular foods. And, no, sticking out his tongue and spitting out the food does not count as an adverse reaction. That's just poor baby table manners.

At first, one solid-food meal a day is plenty. After a few months, your baby will work his way up to eating three meals with different combinations of cereal, fruits, vegetables, yogurt, and meat. When he is around 10 months old, try out small finger foods or table foods that he can pick up and feed to himself.

> CAUTION: *Make sure he's not putting anything into his mouth that's large enough to cause choking. Never give small infants raisins, nuts, popcorn, or small or hard food pieces.*

- **Raising a healthy eater.** Help your baby develop a diet that's as varied and healthy as yours is. Can you make a baby-friendly version of what you're already eating for dinner tonight? You'll save time and broaden your little one's palate. Bravo!

Seven Simple Baby-Food Recipes

Believe it or not, it's easy to make your own baby food with fresh, healthy, and super-affordable ingredients you already have in the kitchen. Here are some of our go-to favorites:

Baby Banana

Peel a very ripe banana. Mash it with a fork. Thin with baby milk as needed.

Yummy Sweet Potatoes

Peel and chop a sweet potato. Bake, boil, or microwave it until soft; allow to cool. Puree in a blender or with a stick mixer until smooth. Thin with baby milk as needed.

Soft Pear

Peel and slice a very ripe pear. Steam it until a fork goes through it easily. Puree until smooth and free of lumps. Thin further with baby milk or thicken with infant cereal.

Avocado

Cut one small avocado in half and remove the pit. Scoop the flesh into a bowl and mash it with a fork. Thin with baby milk as needed. Serve quickly (or it will brown).

Brown Rice Cereal

Grind brown rice in a blender or food processor. Bring 1 cup of water to a boil. Stir ¼ cup of ground rice into the boiling water. Simmer for 10 minutes, whisking constantly. Thin with baby milk or add fruit puree as desired. Serve warm.

Applesauce

Purchase a jar of organic applesauce with no added sugar. Open and serve.

Mushy Peas

Steam a package of frozen peas until soft. Let cool. Puree in a blender or with a stick mixer until smooth. Thin with water or baby milk as necessary.

The Miracle of White Noise

Years ago, moms swore by the whirring sound of a vacuum cleaner to calm their babies. And maybe you've heard a friend talk about driving her baby around in the car to put her to sleep. There's a reason for these noisy tricks.

During pregnancy, the soundtrack of your body surrounds your baby in your uterus, and it's actually quite loud. When our little ones emerge into the world, they miss the noises to which they've become accustomed. When we whisper "shhh" in their ears, we are providing a little taste of that calming tone for which a newborn is homesick.

White noise is an important tool to help calm a fussy baby back to sleep. So where can you get this magic stuff? Here are a few easy sources to consider.

1. **From your mouth.** While holding your baby, make the sound "shhh-shhh-shhh-shhh." Loudly. We have been spotted marching up and down halls, matching our verbal shushing to the rhythm of our steps.

Pro: Always on hand. **Con:** Exhausting.

2. **From the world around you.** The hair dryer, the radio set to static, the old-fashioned vacuum cleaner, and freeway noise in a nonluxury car can all provide the constant white noise that your baby loves. **Pro:** No purchase necessary. **Con:** May produce eco-guilt.

3. **From technology.** White-noise machines, MP3s, and apps for your smartphone or computer have all been designed with peaceful sleep in mind. We highly recommend investing in a plug-in white-noise machine found in most drug stores.

   Pro: Available on demand. **Con:** Costs money, but you'll save on Starbucks when your baby sleeps longer.

How to Take a Baby on an Airplane

Flying as a parent is never quite as relaxing as your memory of those carefree pre-parenting days, when all you had to carry in your purse was a magazine or a book. Now, it's all-hands-on-deck for most of the journey. With just a little planning, you can make the job easier on yourself, your little one, and your fellow passengers.

Before the trip, make two lists of things you'll need: ON THE PLANE and TO PACK. Refer to those lists often as you try to set out of the house. Save your TO PACK list with your suitcase to make repacking, and even future trips, easier. Arrange to borrow bulky items, like a portable crib, at your destination to lighten your load.

Most airlines allow you to wheel a stroller right up to the boarding door and check it beneath the plane at the last possible second. Thank you very much.

To keep your hands as free as possible, use a backpack as your carry-on and fill it with purse essentials and baby must-haves.

Don't forget:

- ☑ Diapers (1 for every hour of travel)
- ☑ Wipes
- ☑ Ointment (Why do babies develop rashes in the middle of a flight? We don't know; just plan for it.)
- ☑ Infant pain reliever
- ☑ A change of clothes
- ☑ Favorite blanket or other security object
- ☑ Burp cloth
- ☑ Pacifier (sucking can help with ear pain on take-off and landing)
- ☑ A few favorite toys and books

Babies who are held in their parents' arms or in a baby-wearing device fly for free. Buying your baby her own seat will allow you to place her in an infant car seat during the trip. The length of your flight and the number of adults in your traveling party may influence your decision whether to hold your baby for the whole flight.

Pro tip: To equalize ear pressure and improve your baby's comfort, try to time feedings with take-off and landing. But since that's nearly impossible, don't be afraid of the pacifier.

How to Sing a Baby to Sleep

Rocking a baby to sleep or helping her settle down in her crib works best when accompanied by a soothing song. No matter how terrible your voice may be, your child will love it. But what to sing?

Here are lyrics to the first verses of four popular night-night songs, along with three that were not intended for sleepyheads but work just as well.

Traditional Lullabies

Twinkle, Twinkle, Little Star

> *Twinkle, twinkle, little star,*
> *How I wonder what you are.*
> *Up above the world so high,*
> *Like a diamond in the sky.*
> *Twinkle, twinkle, little star,*
> *How I wonder what you are.*

You Are My Sunshine

> *You are my sunshine*
> *My only sunshine.*
> *You make me happy*

When skies are grey.
You'll never know, dear,
How much I love you.
Please don't take my sunshine away.

Brahms's Lullaby (a.k.a. Lullaby and Goodnight)

Lullaby, and good night,
With pink roses bedight,
With lilies o'erspread,
Is my baby's sweet head.
Lay you down now, and rest,
May your slumber be blessed!
Lay you down now, and rest,
May thy slumber be blessed!

Rock-a-bye Baby

Rock-a-bye, baby
In the treetop
When the wind blows
The cradle will rock
When the bough breaks
The cradle will fall
And down will come baby
Cradle and all

Not-So-Traditional Lullabies

These three songs can't claim the same long-standing esteem as the classic bedtime soothers, but they're rumored to work just as well: the theme song to the television show *Cheers* a.k.a. "Where Everybody Knows Your Name," "Sweet Child o' Mine" by Guns N' Roses, and "Here Comes the Sun" by the Beatles.

At the end of the day, any song that is sung in a loving tone, accompanied by some pats on the back, will relax your child. Use a search engine to find the lyrics to an old favorite, or have fun making up new words to an old tune to suit your baby. Zzz . . .

Make a Boo-Boo Bunny

When your little one gets a boo-boo, it can be scary. But having a boo-boo bunny come to the rescue can make the whole ordeal much less frightening—especially if she helps you make her little long-eared buddy.

What You'll Need:

- Washcloth
- Rubber band
- Craft glue
- Adornments of your choice (pom-poms, googly eyes, ribbon)

Directions:

1. Lay the washcloth on a flat surface in a diamond shape.

2. Starting with the bottom corner, roll the washcloth up until you reach the middle. Then roll the top corner down to match.

3. Pull the loose ends of the washcloth together, with the rolled-up side facing inward. Fold the loose ends back over the

body, and secure a rubber band to form a head and ears.

4. To finish your bunny, add any adornments you'd like—tie a ribbon around the rubber band, glue on a pom-pom nose and tail, add wiggly eyes. And voilà! Boo-boo bunny! Just slip an ice cube in the center of the body when your little one gets an ouchie, and soon she will feel all better.

How to Stock Your Medicine Cabinet

Childhood is certainly prime time for visits to the doctor, though most day-to-day injuries and illnesses can be treated at home by Dr. Mom. Here is a brief guide to the key ingredients that should be found in every mom's medicine cabinet.

Medications	Also known as
Infants' Tylenol	Acetaminophen
Infants' Motrin	Ibuprofen
Nasal saline	Clean salt water
Gripe water	H_2O with herb extracts and baking soda
Children's Benadryl	Antihistamine

Tip: A well-stocked medicine cabinet will help make all kinds of boo-boos better in a flash.

	Used for
	Pain relief; fever reduction (easier on the tummy)
	Pain relief; fever reduction (lasts longer)
	Stuffy noses
	Upset tummies, hiccups, digestive problems in young babies
	Stuffy noses; itchy conditions such as chicken pox, bug bites, or rashes

Topical Remedy	Also known as
Aquaphor	Petrolatum
Cortaid	Hydrocortisone 1%
Lotrimin	Clotrimazole
Polysporin	Bacitracin

Used for
Healing extra-dry skin, such as nostrils rubbed raw from a cold or irritation caused by drooling
Soothing itchy skin from irritations such as poison oak rashes or insect bites
Relieving itching or burning from cracked skin, cracked nipples, or skin fungi such as ringworm
Preventing infection of minor scrapes and burns

Equipment and First Aid

Supplies	Used For
Thermometer	A digital thermometer that can be used for rectal temperature is good for young babies. Ask your pediatrician or nurse to show you how to use it.
Nail clipper	Tiny versions are sold for little fingers and toes.
Nasal aspirator	For sucking boogers out of little noses.
Tweezers	For removing splinters.

Supplies	Used For
Syringe	For administering the correct amount of medicine. Always double check the recommended dose on both the package and the syringe. And then check again.
Band-Aids	Available in every color of the rainbow and every cartoon character on television. Keep various shapes and sizes on hand.
Telfa	Nonstick pads to prevent infection of large scrapes.
Tape	For holding nonstick pads in place.
Gauze	For wrapping big owies.

Very Important Paperwork

Not only are parents responsible for the care and feeding of little ones who cannot do these things for themselves, they are also responsible for the finances and future of tiny people who cannot yet open a file cabinet or sign their own names.

- **Don't lose the documents.** After your baby is born, you will have to fill out forms to obtain a birth certificate and a Social Security card. Make three copies of each of these documents and place them all in a file. Whenever you need one, try to use a photocopy. When you run low on copies, make more. You may want to add your child's Social Security number to a secret hiding place in your cell phone so that you have easy access without carrying around the original. You'll need it to open a savings account or college fund, for health insurance, and to claim your new dependent on your taxes.

- **Have baby, will travel.** If your family is the traveling type, get your baby a passport without much delay. It's likely that both parents will need to be present to sign the application, so make an appointment when you're both available. You'll need a birth certificate and Social Security number for this task as well. (If you have no specific travel plans, you may want to wait until your babe is able to hold her head up for the passport photo.)

- **Plan for the future**. Here's the part of this chapter you don't want to think about.

  In the case of your own death, it is important that you and your partner have agreed on the person or persons who should care for your child—and then document your wishes.

  With help from either a computer program or a lawyer, you should produce a will that includes your intentions for your child's guardianship in the case that both parents die. Update these documents whenever your family grows or your plans change. And make sure to inform your intended "just-in-case" guardian of your decision.

- **Life insurance.** Another biggie. Will one parent alone be able to fulfill both the income needs AND the childcare, cooking, and cleaning needs of the family? If not, and life insurance is not provided to you as an employee benefit, consider whether you need to purchase a policy on your own. A financial planner can help with this decision.

How to Meet Other Moms

Finding other moms to connect with is critical to one's mental health. If your existing pool of friends isn't brimming with babies right now, try to meet some new women with whom you can compare notes on feeding, sleeping, not sleeping, and, um, not sleeping.

Places to meet other moms include a first-time-mothers' support group, breast-feeding support group, prenatal and postnatal yoga classes, baby gym and music classes, and library and bookstore storytimes for babies. Show up at the same place week after week, and you'll certainly see some familiar faces.

Need some pickup lines?

"Do you come here often?" is actually relevant and not at all a creepy way to strike up a conversation with another mom when you're trying to get to know a new setting. If you are truly shy, cling to some of these basic conversation starters:

- *"She's so cute! How old is she?"*
- *"I love his shoes. Do you remember where you got them?"*
- *"I have the same [piece of gear] at home but haven't quite figured out how to use it. Can you show me?"*

Go online

The Internet is a new mom's best friend. From discussion boards to mommy blogs to neighborhood e-mail lists, you just might find the support you need, right when you need it. Three phrases to Google:

- "birth club" and the month and year of your child's birthday
- "play group" and the name of your neighborhood or town
- "moms who" and the term you are passionate about, such as "cloth diaper" or "run marathons."

Show your true colors

A sunny disposition is indeed an excellent quality through which to attract new friends; just be sure to keep it real when you do have the chance to talk to other moms. Be brave enough to say things like, "I'm having trouble with X" or "I hope I'm not the only mom here who thinks . . ." and you'll invite a more authentic connection with a like-minded mom.

Baby-Proof Like an Expert

There are baby-proofing professionals who will install gates and latches in your home for a fee, and then there is the common sense that we will share with you for free:

Get down on the floor of each room and see what you can get into from a baby's perspective. What looks dangerous and interesting? What is so tempting you can't refuse to reach for it? Those are the objects and situations you need to fix.

- **Prioritize changes to your house that will save your baby's life.** Start with the most perilous problems and work down from there. For example, lock up hazardous chemicals and strap down a television or piece of furniture that could fall over if pulled. Other "tier one" changes include preventing access to windows and stairs.

  You can choose to leave the rest unguarded, depending on your style of parenting (see page 49). If problem areas might result in only small injuries or annoying clean-ups,

Baby Stuff | 47

Lock up hazardous chemicals.

you can decide how important it is to address them. A small houseplant tipping over is not fatal, just unpleasant. Are you feeling lucky? If so, let it be.

Choking hazards: Babies love to put things in their mouths. Keep small objects like coins, buttons, caps—anything that's small enough to fit inside a cardboard toilet-paper roll—out of their reach.

• **Toddlers are a whole different story.** This time, get down at knee level and see the world from their vantage point. Again, check each room for hazards. Is there anything on the counter that could accidentally be pulled down from this height? Having a new walker in your family means it's probably wiser to cook on the back burners of the stove and keep countertops clear of knives, clutter, and anything that curious hands might want to grab.

Simple contraptions that keep cabinets, drawers, and outlet plugs secure and safe from prying fingers can be purchased at many hardware stores.

Cheat Sheet of Parenting Philosophies and Trends

The terms below are defined for the purposes of helping you keep up with conversation or parenting news stories. For the most part, these labels serve to make mothers judge one another and, worse, judge themselves. So whether you're a gung-ho practitioner of a particular parenting philosophy or a make-it-up-as-you-go-along-er, rest assured that no one will be testing you on this knowledge. Especially not your kids.

- **Authoritarian parenting:** The parent is the leader, makes decisions, and does not need to rationalize to the child. This style of parenting earned media attention under the name "Tiger Mom." (Even if you feel you fall far outside this realm, know that at some point we all are driven to say, "Because I said so!")

- **Authoritative parenting:** The parent provides structure and sets limits, but explains reasons for punishments in an effort to encourage independence. ("We don't throw things because they might hurt someone or something, so I'm going to have you take a break from this toy.")

- **Attachment parenting:** This term is associated with three activities: baby-wearing, co-sleeping, and breast-feeding on demand rather than on a schedule. The philosophy is that children will grow up to be emotionally secure and enjoy higher self-esteem when they learn to separate from their parents at their own pace. Critics point out that this practice is extremely demanding on mothers. ("We don't own a crib. Our baby sleeps with us at night and in a sling during the day.")

- **Free-range parenting:** This movement seeks to preserve the notion that children grow into independence by practicing it. ("Go ride your bike and come home before dinner.")

- **Helicopter parenting:** The underlying assumption of this parent is that the child is fragile and must be protected from the dangers of the world. This habit is so named for the physical resemblance that a parent who hovers over her child has to a helicopter. ("Be careful!")

- **Permissive parenting:** This style of child rearing assumes that loving and bonding with the child is the goal of parenting. This parent doesn't want her child to be mad at her. The parent-child relationship here might be described as a democracy. ("My daughter and I are best friends!")

- **Slow parenting:** Similar to the slow-food movement, the idea behind this philosophy is to stop and smell the roses, to let children set the pace of their day. Playing is their work, and the natural world is the best place for their discoveries and learning to occur. Electronic toys are discouraged because they don't promote exploration. Slow parenting might be interpreted as a backlash to overscheduling children with activities and events. ("We didn't make it to preschool today because we found an interesting pattern of rocks in the garden and spent time studying them.")

Little Kid Stuff

Making a Long Wait Fun

Nowadays, we all have smartphones loaded with apps, videos, and family photos to keep our kid-dos happy. But doesn't it always seem like the longest waits are completely unexpected? The trick is to be prepared, which includes always carrying a pen and scrap paper.

Whether you're standing in a line at a store or waiting for a table at a restaurant, here are a few tricks that can pass the time when the phone battery dies.

- **Finger puppets.** Use a pen to draw some faces on your fingertips and create an impromptu finger-puppet show.

- **Racetrack.** Use that same pen to draw a road or city scene on a piece of paper. Use coins from your purse as cars or characters in the adventure you and your child invent.

- **I spy . . .** Even little kids easily catch on to this fun guessing game. Find an object and provide a hint: "I spy with my little eye, something that is blue," and then

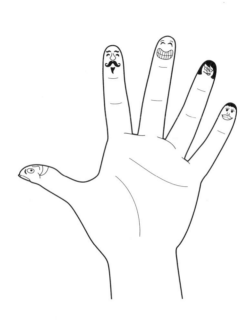

*Draw funny faces on your fingers for an
impromptu finger-puppet show.*

everyone guesses what it is. This oldie but goodie is perfect for waiting rooms and traffic jams.

- **Car games.** See page 119 for a refresher on a few car games that can be modified for standing around.

- **Spoon on the nose.** Need a classy distraction during a long wait at a restaurant? Wipe your thumb across the inside of a metal spoon, breathe hard on it (like you're saying, "HAH!"), then dangle it from your schnoz.

How to Photograph Your Child

The key to capturing your child's age and stage is not necessarily a head-on snapshot with a full smile. Here are five tips that will bring personality, beauty, and visual diversity to your photo albums.

1. **Light it right.** Natural light produces the best-quality photos, so try to avoid using a flash. Look for a shade-free window if indoors or a casual scene outdoors. Kids playing on a grassy field on an overcast day is perfect.

2. **Make a mini studio.** Clear furniture out of the way to make a set for your photo shoot. Arrange one or two props, like a brightly colored chair or a ride-on toy, if your child needs to be contained.

3. **Style your model.** You'd be surprised how distracting a Thomas the Tank Engine top or a Dora-emblazoned dress can be. Opt instead for plain, design-free clothing, like a white snapsuit, jeans and a solid-color T-shirt, or a floral sundress.

The simplicity of the wardrobe will focus attention on your child's adorable mug, rather than those of the cartoons.

4. **Try different angles.** Newborns can be photographed from above. Place a solid-color blanket on your bed and stand over your baby, looking down. Get on your belly to capture your child crawling or playing with toys on the floor.

5. **Focus closer.** Try cropping in on one detail: just the toes of a baby, or just the galoshes of a preschooler.

How to Build a Kickass Blanket Fort

What's easier to build than a tree house? A blanket fort! These makeshift shelters are a snap to set up with materials available in any hotel or grandparent's house. Whether used as a secret place to snuggle together or a quiet nook for your privacy-seeking little one, building a blanket fort is a terrific way to pass a sick day or a rainy afternoon.

Materials

Soft Things	Connectors
blankets	binder clips
bed sheets	rubber bands
pillows	painter's tape
sofa cushions	safety pins

1. **Survey the landscape** and choose an area that's out of the way of traffic but fortified with strong furniture. Your foundation can be a bunk bed, dining table, chairs, or a flipped-over couch.

2. **Begin with the foundation,** spreading the blankets and draping them over other pieces of furniture. Use additional sheets and blankets to add more room inside the fort. A quilt makes a nice cushy floor.

3. **Use connectors** to join sheets and blankets to keep them from falling. Wherever you see sags in the sheets, simply bring in another chair or support to prop up. Wooden clothespins come in handy!

4. **Create a door** so you can enter and exit without having to take apart the whole fort. Leave an opening on the side or prop up a tunnel using couch cushions.

5. **Stock the fort** with necessary supplies— that is, whatever age-appropriate items your kid wants: stuffed animals, snacks, sleeping bags, flashlights, puzzles, books.

6. **Step back and enjoy your awesome creation.** Now it's time to play!

The Truth about Potty Training

For some children, potty training is a simple matter of readiness. They announce their intentions and start using the toilet. If you have one of these children, go ahead and pat yourself on the back.

Other children approach potty training as the most significant power struggle of their young lives. If you have one of these children, welcome to the club.

Here are six truisms about graduating from diapers.

- **You can lead a toddler to the toilet, but you can't make him pee.** Children use the toilet when *they're* ready, not when *you're* ready. Offer easy access to potties and plenty of opportunity, but don't force the issue.

- **Sweatpants and leggings are your friends.** For quick potty runs, toddlers maneuver better in pants they can pull up and down on their own—and quickly.

- **It might get messy.** Anticipating a certain gross-out factor will probably keep your expectations in check. If you manage to escape the poops-in-underwear phase, you're lucky. Remember that your child is learning something new, so try not to shame him for mistakes. Believe it or not, pooping right next to the toilet is progress.

- **The range of normal is broad.** Somewhere between birth and kindergarten, your child will master his bladder's cues. Try not to obsess about whether this is happening "late" or "early."

- **Candy and stickers will get you only so far.** Some children respond really well to a sticker chart that rewards their efforts with a little star. Other children love a well-timed congratulatory M&M. Is your child motivated by big-kid undies or a "No More Diapers" celebration party? Would he be proud to teach a doll how to use the potty? You might have to try a variety of tactics.

- **Nighttime training sold separately.** Wondering when your child will stop needing diapers at night? Between ages 3 and 7 is considered normal. That's pretty wide open, but it should offer you some comfort as you find yourself tossing a package of Pull-Ups into your shopping cart for the same kid who mastered a two-wheeler the weekend before.

Why You Need a Mom's Night Out

One word: sanity.

Of course, we wouldn't trade our children for anything in the world! But after a day of wiping noses and tushies, reconnecting with girlfriends is priceless. If you spend your evening out with mom friends, feel free to talk about the little ones without curious ears around. If you're out with child-free buddies, elevate your game and talk about something *else*.

Go somewhere you used to enjoy in your pre-kid life. Book the time on your calendar and try to make it a recurring event (say, every third Thursday or second Tuesday); that way, you and your pals (and all your respective partners) can plan adequately. If practical, schedule it early enough in the evening so that you escape the entire dinner-slash-bedtime combo back at home.

Wondering what to do with yourself? Try these easy ideas.

Take time out for yourself.

- **Ladies' game night.** Find a pub that serves up Scrabble with the sammies or Boggle with the beer and meet your friends for a few rounds.

- **Wine tasting.** If there's a local winery, a wine bar, or a wine shop that does tastings nearby, make an evening of it! You don't have to live in Napa to taste wine with the gals. But if your town is lacking wine destinations, turn your wine-tasting night out into a night in. Ask each friend to bring a bottle of wine or cheese or other yummy snacks and let your hair down at home!

- **Take a class.** Whether you're foodies or crafters or just plain boisterous, sign up to take a class together. Try cake decorating, pottery, drawing, dancing, improv, or knitting or find a lecture series—use your Mom's Night Out to learn something fun while you catch up with your girlfriends.

- **Find a dive bar.** Put on your lipstick and feel young when you and your gal pals get carded at the local, seedy watering hole. You'll have plenty to giggle about that's not baby-related during your walk on the wild side of town.

- **Spa night in.** Your night out can be at a friend's house too. Rotate hostesses, bring supplies for manis, pedis, and facials, and share classy cocktails and light snacks—all while you lounge, chat, and pamper yourselves. The dress code? Skip the heels and wear comfy pajamas or yoga pants.

- **Book club.** Find new reading material, and discuss current literature. Or forget the book and just use the opportunity to chat and eat dessert!

- **Extended dinner and drinks.** No need to dress the evening up with distracting activities—find a restaurant that will let you sit for hours and chat away.

The primary goal of any night out without the kids is to enjoy some adult conversation and interaction. In addition to the relief of letting your hair down (without someone pulling it), going out with friends is a wonderful way to remember who you are, apart from someone's mommy.

Five Fantastic Outings to Do with Your Toddler

Toddlers are tiny little people with big ideas and lots of enthusiasm. Here are five ways to make the most of both.

1. **Take a hike.** Find a nearby dose of nature and take your little one on a walk. Enjoy the magic of snails and sticks as you walk at her pace. Choose a short trail or bring your off-road stroller.

2. **Tour the hardware store.** Channel your inner dad and visit a place packed with favorites such as door handles, light switches, and fans. Explore the different things to see and touch. Take home some paint chips as a souvenir.

3. **Make the most of the library.** The library is a terrific place to visit for story-time, free books, and a change of pace. Some even offer additional entertainment on the weekends, such as puppet shows. Check out the schedule of the one nearest you.

4. **Exhaust the playground.** Run, climb, and swing until you're both ready for a nap. If you're getting tired of the local action, head outside your own neighborhood for a new adventure at an unfamiliar park.

5. **Reimagine the everyday.** What's boring to you is a never-before-experienced thrill for your child. A simple walk to the mailbox—stopping to explore every sidewalk crack or flower or bug in action—or a ride on the town bus can be truly magical. See the world through your child's eyes and you're sure to be as amazed as she is with the wonder of the world around you.

Five Dates That Don't Require a Babysitter

After you put your babe to bed, go ahead and choose your own adventure!

1. **Sweets.** Share a fancy dessert and wine by candlelight. Make it something decadent, like soufflé or fondue. Stare into each other's eyes and try to talk about things other than parenting.

   Prep work: Pick up supplies earlier in the day.

2. **Game night.** Invite friends over for a double date to play board games or video games. If your friends with children are hard to coordinate with, invite your child-free pals.

   Prep work: Clear the plastic toys off the couch and coffee table.

3. **Home cinema.** Turn an ordinary evening in front of the TV into a date by adding candy and a big bowl of buttery popcorn. With DVRs and online streaming, you don't even need to plan ahead for a movie

rental. Bonus points for those who watch a double feature. *Star Wars*, anyone?

Prep work: A snack run to the convenience store.

4. **Dinner for two.** Reconnect in the kitchen by turning dinner prep with your partner into a fun, sexy time. Enjoy the dance of cooking together and let it last the whole evening long.

Prep work: Agree on a recipe, prepare a romantic playlist, and purchase required ingredients.

5. **Drive out to the drive-in.** Hop in the car—with your baby—and head to the drive-in, if you're lucky to have one nearby.

Prep work: Identify the nearest drive-in, and then drive your baby to sleep before the movie's start time.

Calculate how much you saved by not using a babysitter this time, and treat yourself to child care the next!

Ridding a Bedroom of Monsters

Many children develop fears of creepy things lurking in their rooms at night—especially when they're all tucked up in a bedroom that looks very different from the room they see in the daytime. Shadows, noises, and vivid imaginations can escalate these phobias to the point of robbing everyone in the house of sleep. Here are some ways to tame the wild things.

1. **Assure your child that monsters do not exist.** Explain that they are fictional characters invented to make movies and books more exciting and interesting. Sometimes they are even silly. But just like a cat who wears a hat, they are not real.

2. **Surround her with security objects.** Remind her that if she feels scared, her superpowered teddy bear is right beside her. Offer a push-button nightlight that sticks to any surface (no drilling required!), found at any hardware store. Keep surfaces clear of clutter that, when

the lights are off and shadows emerge, might resemble a scary stranger.

3. **Arm her with monster-be-gone spray.** Many veteran moms report that a magical spritzer can be another effective tool in the arsenal to battle monsters. Crafty moms can have fun with this project: Fill a spray bottle with water and a touch of vanilla extract. Make a special label that says MONSTER SPRAY. If you prefer the store-bought route, try lavender-scented mists intended to calm fussy babies, available from baby-skincare product manufacturers. Let your little one give her sleeping area a squirt to ensure a restful night.

Six Toys Found in Any House

Most homes have lots of hidden toys just waiting to be discovered. This little-known fact can come in handy when visiting your child-free friends, the grandparents, or anyone not equipped with building blocks, stuffed animals, and trucks and trains. Use these six ideas as a starting point for finding the fun in not-so-obvious places.

1. **Masking tape or painter's tape.** Create an indoor hopscotch course, train tracks, or even a tiny city using a little tape and some imagination.

2. **The kitchen sink.** Find a place where it's OK to get a little wet and let your child wash some plastic dishes in a sink or bowl. Have a hose outside? Even better! Put it on a slow trickle and let the splashes begin!

3. **Blankets and pillows.** These can be stacked and draped to create covered fun houses for kids to play in. See page 59 for instructions on making a killer fort.

Never get stuck without playtime activities.

4. **Paper and pens.** Let your little one doodle, draw, practice letters, and solve homemade mazes—just be sure to provide some supervision so that she doesn't damage tabletops, walls, or other surfaces.

5. **DVD cases.** A shelf packed with movies or video games is almost as good as a road or train tracks. Encourage your child to make a path by laying the cases on the living-room floor while the adults sit around drinking coffee.

6. **A set of party cups.** Paper or plastic cups can be used as the building blocks of a pyramid or palace. A younger child can make a stack of three or ten, with some help. An older child can be challenged to see how quickly she can make and unmake the pyramid. (Use a stopwatch, if you dare.)

Healthy Snacks for Kids

Little kids get hungry all the time. Because their tummies are so small, there's no point in putting the kibosh on between-meal snacks for about another ten years. The best thing you can do is have lots of healthy options on hand.

- **Apples and nut butter.** Slice the apples, spread on peanut or almond butter, and serve with an extra helping of napkins.

- **Fruit smoothie.** Place frozen fruit, bananas, and yogurt in a blender and process till smooth. Serve with an extra-wide straw.

- **Hummus and pita.** Spread hummus onto triangles of whole wheat pita or let your child dip the pita in the hummus. If your child is older, offer carrot sticks, too.

- **Sunflower seeds and raisins.** Great for a stroller snack, this modified trail mix can be eaten straight from the bag.

- **Cheese and cherry tomatoes.** Cheese sticks, cubes, shreds, or circles provide a good boost of calcium and protein. Pair cheese with small tomatoes for sweetness.

Ostriches Are as Fast as a Car, and Other Fun Animal Facts

Kids love animals, and they love facts perhaps just as much. Combine the two, and you have a winner. Keep a few of these facts in your noggin—and research even more on the Internet—to impress your preschooler everywhere you go.

- Ostriches can run as fast as a car, topping out at speeds of 43 miles per hour.

- When giraffes are born, they are 6 feet tall (point to yourself as a visual clue) and can walk the first day of their lives.

- Sharks may grow and use over 20,000 teeth in a lifetime, and they have up to 3,000 teeth in their mouths at any one time.

- Sloths hang upside down, even while eating.

- Penguins can jump up to 6 feet high.

- Armadillos have 4 identical babies at a time, sometimes all male, sometimes all female, but never a mix of the two.

- The smallest hummingbirds flap their wings 80 times per second.
- The puffer fish makes itself too big to swallow by ingesting water and puffing up.
- A cockroach can live several weeks with its head cut off, though it will eventually die of starvation.
- All polar bears are left-handed.
- Butterflies smell with their feet.
- Elephants can't jump.
- Oysters change from male to female several times during their lifespan.
- Zebras are white with black stripes.
- You can lead a cow up the stairs, but not down the stairs.
- Squirrels accidentally plant millions of trees by burying their nuts and forgetting where they are.

Get Your Child to Dress Herself

Maybe it's that kids like to be in control, maybe it's that they don't like things being pulled over their heads—but either way, getting dressed in the morning can be a daily struggle! The most important thing to remember when trying to get your child into her clothes is to establish a routine. Make sure to get her dressed at the same time every day: first thing, after breakfast, whenever works. A routine will help her understand that getting dressed is just a part of starting the day.

Tips to Help Get Your Child Dressed:

- **Let her pick her clothes**—with guidance of course. It'll make her feel like she's a part of the process.

- **Buy shirts that are easy to put on**—tops that button up or have wide collars—so you don't have to pull tight shirts over her head.

- **Turn getting dressed into a race:** "Quick! We have to get you dressed before Daddy sees you! Hurry, he's coming . . ." or "Let's see if we can get you dressed by the time I count to twenty."

- **Teach your child to get dressed by herself.** Tape pictures of clothing on her dresser drawers so she knows where to find everything she needs.

- **Give her a choice:** "Do you want to wear this outfit or that outfit?" or "Do you want to put your pants on first or your shirt?"

- **Turn getting dressed into a role-playing activity.** Turn her bedroom into a chic boutique and pretend to be a salesperson while she shops. Suggest different items and let her choose. And don't forget to make her pay at the end!

Fifteen Birthday-Party Survival Tips

Who doesn't love a birthday party? They are definitely fun but can also be exhausting, expensive, and stressful. Oftentimes, the tricks that save effort—like hosting the party at an all-inclusive playspace—cost a ton, whereas those that save money have you up all night painting, baking, and covered in papier-mâché.

By focusing on the parts of party planning and hosting that you truly enjoy, you'll be able to turn a potentially stressful endeavor into a fun afternoon for your child and her friends. Here are a few recommendations from the party-planning trenches.

Sanity Savers

1. Plan and do as much as you can beforehand to avoid last-minute scrambles. Eight weeks before the party, agree on a date, the number of invitees, and the venue (home, restaurant playspace, state park, traveling reptile show at the local natural-history museum, etc.).

2. Skip the traditional party and bring a few kids on a special outing, for example, a game of mini golf or a new movie followed by dessert.

3. Order the necessities online (pirate loot, custom cake toppers, that one big present).

4. Throw your party on Sunday to give yourself a prep day on Saturday.

5. Say "yes" to offers of help. Your helpers can oversee a craft, run a game, or pass out cake. Assign a guest to take pictures and record the video so you don't have to worry about saving the memory in a shareable format.

Time Savers

1. Decorate simply with colorful bunches of helium-filled balloons.

2. Save on prep by making your activity the party favor: decorate picture frames, fill flowerpots, or bead necklaces together.

3. Eliminate the cake, which requires slicing and forks. What about a tower of doughnuts decorated with flowers or a tray of cupcakes with sprinkles on top?

4. Create thank-you notes before the party, with the birthday child, so that they're all ready to mail once the gifts have been opened and the guests have gone home.

5. Outsource the food: order pizza, pick up a deli tray, or ask Grandma to make her specialty.

Money Savers

1. Schedule the party during non-meal time; serve healthy snacks before dessert.

2. Limit the guest list.

3. Buy solid-color paper goods on sale or at the discount store.

4. Use an online invitation rather than printed ones.

5. Eliminate party-favor bags.

Five Fun Projects to Do with Your Preschooler

Preschoolers are an imaginative bunch. Harness that creativity to pass a fun afternoon together. All that's required to create something new is a few raw materials and some inspiration.

1. **Design a cardboard playhouse.** Take the biggest box in your house and invite your child to become an architect. Tape on additional boxes to create more interior space and then cut holes for windows and flaps for doors. Use stickers, paint, or markers to decorate your playhouse together. Design the interiors, too, or just settle down to a game of house.

2. **Cut up some felt food.** Imagine a menu together of "buildable" foods: salads, sandwiches, tacos, pizza, or something else. Cut colored felt (found at craft stores) into a variety of shapes, assemble your "foods," and enjoy! Nom nom.

3. **Bake something yummy.** Choose a favorite recipe and work as a team to measure, mix, and pour. Point out how

ingredients change as they cook. Then, the best part: eat!

4. **Create a countdown paper chain.** What's the next big event that your kiddo is looking forward to? A birthday? Grandma's visit? A favorite holiday? No event is too small to create a paper countdown chain. Cut as many strips of colored paper as there are days remaining, link them all together with a stapler or tape, and watch the anticipation build as you remove a link on each new day. Can't wait!

5. **Build a recyclo-bot.** Gather up trinkets and recyclables and transform them into a kid-size robot buddy. Build the bot's head from a small box and some yogurt containers and improvise from there. Give a name to your new creation.

*Turn your recyclables into a kid-size
friend for your child.*

How to Raise a Good Citizen

Since many of the tasks we perform today are done on a computer, it's become increasingly harder to teach our children by setting a positive example. They probably don't see us paying our bills, volunteering for snack duty, or helping a friend in need.

So it's important to find opportunities to demonstrate how to help others, perform civic duties, and be an all-around good person. Focus on starting small, in your own house, and then move outward to the community and, ultimately, the planet.

Here are eight simple ways to involve your child in social responsibility:

- Talk as a family when choosing charitable donations and volunteer activities.

- Sort through toys together and make a pile to donate to a local charity or recycling center.

- Prepare and deliver food to a neighbor who's a senior without a car, feeling under the weather, or experiencing a financial rough patch.

- Teach your child to reuse, reduce, and recycle.
- Participate in a local clean-up day.
- Organize a canned-foods drive, coat drive, or diaper drive on behalf of a local shelter.
- Take your child with you to the polls on Election Day.
- Collect loose change and then decide on a cause to which you donate your small savings.

Big Kid
Stuff

Five Special Places to Go with a Grade-Schooler

With extracurricular activities and a busy social life, it can be hard to make time to just be together. Need some inspiration for a special mom-and-kid date? Here are five unexpected places to take off to together.

1. **Factory.** Do you live near a chocolate or jellybean or chip factory? Or maybe another, less-tasty form of manufacturing, such as tools or textiles? Many factories give public tours, and both you and your grade-schooler will learn something new—and maybe get a sample to taste at the end of the tour.

2. **Restaurant.** Change out of your play clothes and venture out on the town for a quiet meal in the dining establishment of your choice. Treat the lunch, brunch, breakfast, whatever like a true special occasion, complete with conversations about topics you both are interested in.

3. **Getting physical.** Playing putt-putt, swinging bats at the batting cages, kicking

*Hands-on museums equal playtime
with education sneaked in.*

a soccer ball in the park—games and exercise give you a chance to cheer each other on and be competitive, too. Round out the match with a little ice cream to soothe any bruised egos.

4. **Museum.** A hands-on science museum, aquarium, children's museum, or special section within an art museum reserved just for kids equals playtime with education sneaked in. The trick is to keep the visits short; when fidgeting breaks out, it's time to call it quits.

5. **Sporting event.** Attend local college or high school games. Popular sports may be more affordable at this level, and those that draw fewer crowds, such as track or swimming, may be free.

Comebacks for Unsolicited Parenting Advice

Sometimes a well-meaning stranger cannot help but tell you that your little one should be wearing a hat, not sucking on your keys, drinking prune juice, etc., etc. Other times, advice that you just don't need comes from someone you love, like your mother or best friend. In either case, it's tough to acknowledge the good intentions of the intruder while rejecting the suggestion altogether.

Of course, you can always respond with, "That's interesting; maybe I'll try it out." But, frankly, if there's no way in Hades you're going to try the proposed method, then find a way to comment on the idea without involving yourself.

"Really? That sounds cool."

"I'm glad that's working for you."

"I've never thought about it that way."

Most of this unsolicited advice is not meant to insult you; it's usually just other people's way of

dusting off their own experiences and passing it off as wisdom.

When it comes to true interference, however, you may be forced to assert yourself as the authority. Another parent at the playground removing your child from a scuffle? Your brother threatening a time-out for your preschooler? Your mother-in-law telling your child she must eat something?

Simply say, "Hey, I've got it." And then handle it.

This is a clear and powerful way to redirect the situation so that you are the one in charge while letting the interfering person know that, well, you are the one in charge.

Dealing with Lice

Lice outbreaks can happen to anyone. These itchy creepy-crawlies like clean as well as dirty scalps and can strike on any hair length. Here's what you need to know.

A vocab lesson:

Eggs are eggs. Nits are partially mature eggs (louse teenagers, if you will) and resemble a sesame seed in color and size. A live nit will have a small black dot in the center. A louse is a small wingless insect that burrows into hair to start a life and build a family; it crawls from head to head and can survive for a brief time off the head while looking for a new home.

To get rid of lice, you'll need to treat the hair and your home at the same time. For the hair, many effective commercial and home remedies are available, ranging from totally toxic to completely natural (including, we kid you not, a mayonnaise hair mask). Talk with your pediatrician about currently recommended products and follow the instructions carefully.

Once you've applied the treatment to the lice-ridden head, your best defense is combing. Thorough and frequent combing, a.k.a. nitpicking, will find and remove all tiny bugs and nits. If you're really good, you'll get the eggs, too.

For a proper comb-through:

1. Separate the hair into sections using hair clips and rubber bands.

2. Using a very fine-toothed nit comb, start immediately next to the scalp and comb to the end of the hair.

3. Flick the comb's contents into a sink to assess the seriousness of the infestation. You may find nits and bugs alongside lint and dandruff.

4. Repeat until all sections of hair have been thoroughly combed.

5. Sterilize your lice-checking tools in boiling water or an alcohol bath.

Continue combing infested heads twice per day for eight days after you no longer see live bugs. If you find more eggs, nits, or bugs, restart the clock. Lice are highly contagious, so be sure to examine noncontaminated heads in your household once per day.

To clear up your home:

Go on a laundry rampage, washing items in hot water and drying them on high heat. Pay special attention to clothes and linens. Treat pillows/pillowcases together each morning and at night by placing them in a hot dryer for 20 minutes. Quarantine any oversized or unwashable stuffed animals or throw pillows in a sealed plastic bag for one week. Without access to a cozy head, lice will die off.

To prevent lice:

Use what the experts use: create or purchase a solution of pure peppermint or tea tree oil mixed with water at a ratio of five drops of essential oil to one cup of water. Spritz this mixture onto your children's hair, hats, coats, and backpacks to prevent infestation. This spray will repel lice and is useful to have on hand when you are notified that your child has been exposed.

Girl, You're a Soccer Mom Now

Enrolling your child in a sports program is a rite of passage. Whether you are hoping your child will follow in your goal-kicking footsteps or simply develop the ability to lose with grace, it's beyond charming to see those little peanuts in their uniforms for the first time. Be it Tee Ball or soccer, here are some things to remember:

1. **Lounge chairs.** If your child's game is played on a small-scale field, chances are you'll want to be closer than the bleachers. Bring your own seating so that you can sit back comfortably and watch the action. A camping chair designed for two tushes allows a pair of spectators to enjoy the action together.

2. **Water.** Fill a sports bottle for your kid (and each spectating member of your family). A spray bottle that delivers a mist to your little athlete's face provides a novel way to cool down.

3. **Sunscreen.** Apply to your child's skin before leaving home and reapply every

thirty minutes or so if your player is sweaty. Protect your skin, too, and don't be afraid to ask another parent to warn you if the back of your neck is turning pink.

4. **Entertainment.** It doesn't make you a bad mom if watching drills bores you. Keep reading material in your bag, and, if you are toting along other children, you'll want to have something for them to do as well. Bubbles or toys will make everyone happier.

5. **Shade.** If you find yourself at an all-day tournament, set up a canopy and you will quickly become the most popular person on the sidelines. On long hot days, a cooler with icy drinks and snacks will seal your reputation as everyone's favorite person.

6. **Ball or mitt.** Warm-up activities often require a piece of equipment for every child. Having her very own soccer ball may also get your kiddo more excited about the activity.

7. **Après-game shoes.** A pair of flip-flops or Crocs is nice to have in the car for after the game. Your child's little feet can get

sweaty and/or muddy. Bag up the sporting shoes and slip on clean, dry footwear.

8. **Camera.** Tote your video capture device once or twice per season. Weekly footage is not necessary at this level. For video tips at the event see page 140.

9. **Snacks.** Sometimes snacks are provided, and sometimes the provider will be you. If the traditional orange slices are going to be distributed, don't forget the wipes. Those juicy treats are sticky. On snack duty? Bring a trash bag to collect peels and wrappers, too.

10. **Blankets.** Chilly weather requires cozy layered clothing and enough blankets to make you comfortable in wet grass, wind, or snow.

Don't leave home without your exemplary attitude. Cheer the whole team on, stay in your seat, and remember to root for your athlete with an encouraging smile when she makes contact with the ball, because the next thing she'll do is look for Mom's approval.

Ten Tricks to Make Dinner Fast

Dinnertime for busy families on school nights is best described as managed chaos. But once you have a few tricks up your sleeve, everyone will marvel at how you get it all done. Here are ten tips to making dinner in 25 minutes or less.

1. **Plan the week ahead.** Analyze your family's evening schedules to determine which meals fit best on which days. If you like to do "one big shop," use up your most perishable ingredients earlier in the week. And never, ever, be afraid of leftovers.

2. **Tackle tasks when you can.** If you find yourself with a few free moments in the day, take advantage of them and chop veggies or start a slow cooker.

3. **Have a few surefire go-to meals.** Based on your skills and your family's tastes and preferences, know what you can whip up in a breeze. Quesadillas, frittatas, and soup and salad are quickie meals that please most palates and use up fresh or frozen veggies. See page 135 for

easy meals that hungry teens (and frazzled moms) can make in a flash.

4. **Love your freezer.** Whether it's a favorite frozen pizza or extra stew from last week, make active use of your freezer to aid with easy meal prep. Thaw leftovers the day before for best results.

5. **Organize for success.** Set up your kitchen for easy access to frequently used appliances and prep stations. Store what you don't use regularly.

6. **Go raw.** Sliced veggies with hummus, fancy caprese salad, and cold cuts wrapped in a pita all count as healthy meals. Whole foods arranged in a clever way on the plate will make you look like a rockstar.

7. **When in doubt, boil water.** If you walk into the house at 6:05 with no clue what's for dinner, boil some water while you contemplate. It can be used for pasta or veggies and will be ready once you make up your mind.

8. **Practice, practice, practice.** With experience comes a whole arsenal of tricks and techniques that will work for your kitchen

and your family. Next time your parents come over to help you make dinner, you'll wonder why they move so slowly.

9. **Make extra.** When you brown ground meat for one meal, make enough to save for another. That way, when you're crunched for time later in the week, you can have a skillet meal, tacos, or a meaty spaghetti dish ready in minutes!

10. **Ask your child to help.** Bigger kids can make salad, set the table, carry over dishes or pour drinks while you prepare the meal. Smaller children can be sent on a mission in another room to keep them from hanging on your leg in the kitchen—"hey sweetie, can you finish this puzzle before dinner?"

How to Make Mickey Mouse Pancakes

1. Prepare pancake batter as usual, from scratch or a box.

2. Using a small ladle or measuring cup, create one round pancake in the center of the griddle. This one will be Mickey's head.

3. As soon as the edges of your first pancake have stopped expanding, pour two smaller circles of batter on the griddle, one on each side of the head, at 10 and 2 o'clock. These will be the ears. (If on your first attempt the ears don't connect with the head, simply flip them as regular pancakes and try again.)

4. When all the bubbles in the three circles have stopped popping, flip the entire shape.

Bonus points for serving fruit that can be used to give Mickey eyes and a nose.

Pro tip: For even greater control, use a turkey baster as a batter dispenser. Heck, you may even feel capable of adding a bow to make Minnie Mouse!

How to Get Chewing Gum Out of Hair

An inevitable misadventure—your kid gets gum stuck in his hair. And not just stuck, wadded into a tangled heap of stickiness. Pulling at it only makes it worse, so resist that temptation. Don't panic, and follow these simple instructions.

1. **Think Fast.** Either grab a prepared ice pack or make one by putting ice cubes in a plastic bag and sealing it closed.

2. **Freeze it.** Pull the sticky hair away from your child's scalp and hold the ice pack against the gum until it is frozen solid, about 15–30 minutes. (Be sure to have rubber gloves or a washcloth handy to keep your fingers from going numb.)

3. **Divide and conquer.** Break the frozen gum into pieces and gently remove them from his hair. If the warmth from your hands starts to thaw the gum and make it sticky again, reapply the ice pack to refreeze the wad.

Here are three other mom-tested remedies to try, starting with the easiest and cleanest:

- **Cooking oil.** Slick out the goo with something slippery.
- **Peanut butter.** Glob some creamy peanut butter around the entanglement, wait a few minutes, and then comb out the greasy mess.
- **Scissors.** Cutting out a nugget of hair and gum is an appropriate choice under these circumstances.

Choose your favorite remedy based on the quantity of gum; the length and texture of hair; and the products you have on hand. You're a superhero mom, so make sure he knows it!

Three Easy Card Games

A deck of cards can make a long rainy day bearable. Know the rules to a few simple games and get the fun started. Here are three kid-friendly options:

1. **War (2 players).** Shuffle the deck and deal all the cards facedown. Don't look at your cards. At the same time, players flip the top card. High card wins both cards, which go to a new pile for each player's winnings. If both players' cards have the same value, players go to "war" by placing two cards facedown and then one card faceup; high card wins all of the cards in the war. The short way is to play once through the deck and then count who has the most cards. The long way is to play until one of you runs out of cards completely (in which case you reshuffle the winnings pile and keep starting over).

2. **Memory, a.k.a. Concentration (2 to 6 players).** For little players, start by eliminating all cards greater than seven. Lay the cards in a grid, for example 4 cards

by 6 cards (if you're using 24 cards). Each player takes a turn turning over two cards, trying to find matching numbers; if cards do not match, the player returns them to their original facedown position. The player who makes a match collects the match and has another turn. Keep matched cards in a faceup pile for each player. The player with the most matches wins.

3. **Go Fish (3 to 6 players).** Shuffle the deck and deal out five cards to each player. The rest of the cards go facedown into the fish pond. The first player asks for a card of a certain number, for example, "Do you have any sixes?" If the answer is yes, that player gives up all the cards of that number; if the answer is no, that player says, "Go fish," and the asker draws a card from the fish pond. If the asker receives the desired cards, she may go again. Once all four of a kind are matched, the player will lay them down in her personal pile. The player with the most sets wins. An easier version of this game allows players to lay down pairs rather than full sets.

Ten Last-Minute Halloween Costumes

There are at least two scenarios that will have you scrambling for a costume without warning. The first is when Halloween sneaks up on you while your child is too young to give you fair warning. *October thirty-first, you say? Wasn't it just Labor Day?* The second is a late-breaking confession from a tween or teen that he or she does want to dress up after all.

With a few accessories and a little imagination, clothing that's already in your drawers can be converted into an ensemble that passes for a costume. What could be greener—or cheaper?

1. **Farmer:** Got overalls? Add a plaid shirt and a bandana and head on out to the hoedown.

2. **Ballerina:** Pink tights under a pink leotard. Finish it off with a pair of flats.

3. **Superhero:** Fashion a cape from a towel or pillow case. Cut wristbands from a discarded long-sleeved shirt. Add a first-initial emblem for extra credit. She's ready to fly!

*Cut the sleeves off an old long-sleeved shirt
to make superhero wristbands.*

4. **Fried egg:** White clothing head to toe with a yellow circle stuck to the midsection. Craft the yolk from felt, paper, or paint.

5. **Tourist:** When else is that Hawaiian shirt your mother gave him going to be appropriate? Hang a pretend camera around his neck and call it a day.

6. **Construction worker:** Have a collection of pretend tools? Hook them to a belt or wear them in the pockets of overalls. Send Mr. Fixer-Upper out the door.

7. **Grapes:** Blow up ten green balloons and tie them to a string. Wrap the string around chest and waist. (Remove for car rides.) Add some felt or paper "leaves" for a full fruity effect.

8. **Celebrity:** Sunglasses and a Starbucks cup will get you halfway there. Identify a notable characteristic of a current headline-maker and apply it to your child.

9. **Athlete:** Baseball and soccer uniforms can be passed off for costumes, especially if they originally belonged to an idolized older sibling or neighbor.

10. **"Smartie" pants:** A classic costume for any age. Glue a handful of Smarties candies to a pair of old pants. Done.

Easy homemade costumes aren't just for Halloween. They're great fun for sleepovers, playdates, and rainy days.

How to Teach a Kid to Cook

At some point between birth and leaving your house for the big bad real world, your child will need to be able to cook a few things. By involving him in some simple steps of food preparation, you're setting him on the path to never going hungry.

Tips for you:

- **Make sure there's enough time.** Not every mealtime is the ideal co-cooking experience. Having company over in ten minutes? Need to whip up a perfect soufflé? Pick a different day.

- **Create a safe environment.** A misshapen pizza or lumpy meatloaf is still edible. Don't sweat imperfection. Support the process by aiming low so no one's disappointed. And remember to keep smiling.

- **Invite input.** Does your child want to add olives to his homemade lemonade? That's a great idea—in his own glass. Encourage his suggestions for flavor combinations. If the food doesn't taste great, talk about what might have happened so you can both learn. Is it too salty? Too spicy? Help him develop his taste buds as well as his opinions.

Kitchen tasks for your child:

- **Break an egg.** Have him do this into a small bowl first so you can more easily fish out broken shells or discard a bad egg without ruining the dish.

- **Measure and dump.** For baking projects, use an intermediate bowl if your child is less than accurate.

- **Whisk and stir.** Introduce the whisk and wooden spoon early in your child's life and prevent your own carpal tunnel syndrome.

- **Tear lettuce.** Your child can own the salad by washing, drying, and ripping lettuce leaves.

- **Spread the goo.** A safe spreading knife can handle butter, hummus, peanut butter, jelly, and a lot more!

- **Set and clear.** Give your child the job of setting and clearing the table to teach him that these tasks don't just happen by themselves.

School-aged kids are capable of tackling many steps of meal preparation. The big question is whether you're patient enough to work together (and keep a smile on your face). If you create a safe learning environment in the kitchen, you may find that eventually your sous-chef will invite you to watch TV while he makes the meal.

Road-Trip Games

Not everyone has the luxury of a movie theater on wheels. And even if you do, sometimes enough is enough and it's time to turn off the screen. Here are seven simple car games to keep the kids engaged and the parents alert.

1. **Basic alphabet search game.** Look for letters in alphabetical order. For A, you might see an Applebee's or an Acme moving truck. For B, who can spot the BP sign first? And on and on through Z. Your carload can work in cooperative or competitive mode, based on ages and temperaments.

2. **Alphabet memory game.** This tricky game is played in a round with all travelers. Take turns working through the alphabet by adding to the story. Start with something like "I'm going on a trip and I'm putting in my suitcase an Apple." The next person might say an apple and a bagel. Continue adding to the loot in alphabetical order, with each person naming an object and remembering what's

gone before, such as an apple and a bagel and a calendar and a doughnut and so on until someone forgets.

3. **Alphabet story game.** A bit easier than the alphabet memory game, this version has each person finding creative words for only their assigned letter. Begin with "A my name is Anna, my husband's name is Al, we live in Arizona, and we sell Apples." The next passenger takes on the letter B and makes a silly sentence using the same basic structure. And so on.

4. **Seated Simon Says.** Using hands and voices, Simon Says is a bit limited but can still be hilarious. "Simon says clap your hands. Simon says wiggle your fingers and pat your belly." This game works best when played with multiple kids.

5. **License-plate hunt.** Best for kids who can read, this game involves keeping track of all the license plates you find from different states. Who can find the most? Winner!

6. **Imaginary hide and seek.** Kids silently choose a place in the house where they are hiding—say, the shower—and the

driver describes walking through the house and trying to find them. "Are you in the kitchen? No? I'm walking up the stairs . . . is that a good decision?" Little ones laugh and squeal as if you're really hunting for them.

7. **Counting.** Pick an object you're seeing frequently out the window, such as windmills, sheep, or a specific make of car, and start counting. Who can find the most of the chosen object? Simple, yes, but hard to stop.

Are we there yet?

Tween Stuff
and Beyond

Five Things to Do with Your Tween That You'll Both Actually Enjoy

Tweens and teens are a tricky bunch. You might think only a crazy person would hate a luxury resort in Hawaii, but, if you go there, you'll surely see adolescents moping around as if they're trapped in the Most Boring Place on Earth.

Here are five ideas for spending time with a teenager that may facilitate some parental bonding—and even some smiles. That is, if he agrees to be seen with you.

1. **Indulge in amusements.** Miniature golf, go-cart racing, arcades, paint-balling, and full-scale amusement parks are outings that will allow you to be a kid again—and your teen to mock you for it. Bonding accomplished.

2. **Pick a flick.** Emerging from a two-hour cinema experience together may encourage good conversation at lunch afterward.

3. **Share a hobby.** Take a pottery class together, learn to play his favorite video game, or go to local sporting events.

4. **Redecorate.** Giving your teen's bedroom a makeover with a D.I.Y. project is an offer he can't refuse. Spend time together painting the room, assembling a piece of furniture, or creating a massive wall display to reflect interests or awards.

5. **Venture outdoors.** Riding bikes or hiking trails allows you to see new things together and take turns navigating. Since you'll be off the beaten path, it reduces the odds that his friends will see you together.

Any activity that enables you and your teenager to work as a team or enjoy a shared experience can infuse your relationship with a shot of joy.

How to Psyche Up for the Tough Talks

Many of us have awkward memories of the times our own parents tried to talk with us about sex, alcohol, and other tough topics. Maybe we vowed to do the opposite when we finally became parents. Regardless, these conversations feel different when you're the mom.

When talking with your child about any difficult topic, the key is to start early and keep the dialogue going. Try to create an open, honest environment. Think of these discussions as preventative medicine. You don't want to introduce your values or expectations for the first time after a mistake has been made.

Here are some tips to get you through it:

- **Initiate the conversation.** As the adult, this is part of your job.
- **Share your feelings, but not your personal experience.** This is not a moment to be buddies; you are providing leadership. Be honest but not graphic.

- **Listen as much as you talk.** Answer the questions your child is asking without providing extra information that she may not need or be ready for.

- **Communicate your values.** Use "I" statements, such as "I feel" or "I believe," to share your viewpoint.

- **Use everyday opportunities** as a springboard for talking: television, music, the news, and her friends.

Hopefully, the conversations you have won't be totally cringe-worthy and can be a good foundation for more meaningful talks in the future. Odds are good that you'll have many chances to practice these skills.

Stock Your House for School Success*

No mom wants to run out to the store at 11 p.m. on a Sunday night because her child has suddenly remembered she needs forty cupcakes in the morning—or, worse, a poster board illustrating the life and times of the Mayan people.

Here are some strategies that will improve your child's ability to complete school assignments on time:

1. **Plan ahead.** Sit down together on Sunday evenings and review the coming week's activities and deadlines. Place reminders in multiple places to improve your odds of remembering events. Use each area of study or interest as the guide to your conversation. For example: "What's coming up in Spanish? What needs to be done for Student Government? Is your soccer uniform clean? How are you getting to Holden's birthday party?"

---

* And avoid a midnight Target run.

2. **Make yourself available.** To reduce requests to get something done *right now*, tell your child exactly when you're available or planning to go to the store, do laundry, be home for homework help, etc. Put time in your own schedule to help with getting supplies, reviewing school assignments, and exploring new activities together. We'd bet that behind every United States president, there's a mom who filled out a whole bunch of summer-camp registration forms.

3. **Keep useful materials on hand.** A study area for your child should include art supplies, scissors, writing tools, colored papers, and whatever is required for major school reports, such as folders or page protectors. Your student needs a place to be creative, away from video games and other distractions, and the tools to do her work. As a child's room requires less toy storage, consider adding a desk where a dollhouse used to be.

How to Keep Your Kids Safe Online

Just as you'll expect your child to behave a certain way at school, a family gathering, or a beach party, how she behaves online also requires etiquette. Is talking to strangers okay? Is sharing a photograph of her prom dress with her friends off-limits? How about a video of her soccer team's pillow fight or the fact that she's currently waiting at the bus stop on Main Street?

Here are some factors to consider when you establish rules for using a computer or handheld device.

- **Think about the future.** Your child needs to understand that every move she makes online is creating an Internet footprint. Future employers can search for a candidate's name and browse results—including pictures and posts—from a variety of sources. Inspire your teen to maintain a profile of which she can be proud.

- **Be smart about scams.** Teach her never to respond to e-mail requests from strangers for money, photographs, passwords, or other personal information.

- **Mind your manners.** Gossip that is forwarded to others can never be retrieved. Encourage your kid to think twice before sending out any message that might hurt another person's feelings.

- **Location, location, location.** Some phones and mobile devices use technology to include specific locations as part of the information shared along with a status update or photo. On one hand, such features allow you to keep tabs on your teen. On the other hand, she may unintentionally be broadcasting her whereabouts to strangers. Consider your comfort level with such features and investigate if it's possible to disable them.

- **Follow house rules.** Agree on the hours when technology can be used and the types of activities that are allowed.

- **Protect and respect.** Many options exist for parental controls; for example, you may be able to protect your child from encountering inappropriate content in search results. Discuss together the benefits of filtering certain content so that your child feels protected rather than controlled.

• **What's in a name?** Select user names that don't reveal important identifying details, such as real name, location, gender, age. Instead, opt for a nickname or a reference to a hobby or favorite activity. Alphanumeric is safe, too. Good examples are JPT3chess or luvs2read.

How to Hug Your Teen without Her Knowing

Little kids are extremely snuggly compared to their cold-shouldered teenage selves. How can a mom get and give the needed hugs each day while avoiding eye-rolling and the sound of a dramatic "MOTHER!"? Sneak them in, of course.

Here are five clever ways to get some physical affection from your kid when she no longer fits in your lap.

1. **Curl up under a blanket together to watch a TV show or movie.** You may need to cut the thermostat by a few degrees to encourage this artful snuggling, but it's worth it.

2. **Pat her on the back.** Think of a genuine compliment for something your teen has been working hard to do, and accompany your praise with pats on the back until she makes you stop.

3. **Work on some dance steps.** Do you know the secret to a waltz or square dance?

Can you pass on your knowledge of the tango? If not, take the time to learn a new physical skill and share it with your child.

4. **Bake cookies.** A kitchen project might have you rubbing shoulders by the stove. That's almost a hug.

5. **Creep in after bedtime.** Tiptoe into the bedroom for one last goodnight kiss or hug after lights-out (or before sunrise, if your teen is a night owl), which might be the least confrontational time of the day.

Three Foods Your Teen Should Be Able to Cook

Some children love to cook and absorb the lessons from their heritage over a mixing bowl and a kitchen timer. For others, you'll be lucky if they can toast bread and boil water before they leave the house for their own first apartments.

Here are three simple recipes your teen should be able to make independently:

Scrambled Eggs

1. Assemble ingredients: 2 eggs, cooking fat (either oil or butter). Crack the eggs into a deep bowl.

2. Warm the fat in a nonstick pan over medium-low heat while whisking the eggs in the bowl. Seventy-five strokes quickly around the bowl will incorporate lots of air and yield the "perfect scrambled eggs."

3. Pour egg mixture into heated pan. Stir frequently with a spatula. Cook to desired consistency.

Grilled Cheese

1. Assemble ingredients: 2 slices of bread, cheese, butter. Butter the outsides of the bread.

2. Place a nonstick pan over medium heat. Assemble the sandwich in the heated pan: bread butter-side down, cheese, bread butter-side up.

3. Press on the sandwich with the back of a spatula. Flip the sandwich after 3 minutes. Smoosh it again. After 3 to 5 minutes, it will be perfect.

Spaghetti

1. Assemble ingredients: dry noodles, tomato sauce from a jar. Fill a big pot three-quarters full with salted water; bring to a boil over high heat.

2. Add noodles and cook for about 8 to 10 minutes. Meanwhile, microwave some sauce for about 1 minute: use a microwave-safe bowl with a paper towel over the top to prevent splattering.

3. Test the noodles for doneness: throw one at the wall and see if it sticks (but just one, please; this is not a food fight!). When they are done, drain them in a colander, pour them back into the pot, and toss with the sauce before serving.

How to Put a Positive Spin on Your Negative Feelings

Because you mostly want to set a good example for your kids—teaching them to solve problems without being rude or nasty—it's important to have some catchphrases in your back pocket. And maybe even a few white lies.

When . . .	Say . . .
you secretly think other adults are bad parents, instead of saying, "Charlie's mom is an idiot."	"I don't agree with Charlie's mom's decision."
you resent your own parents or in-laws, instead of saying, "Grandma is driving me crazy."	"I see things differently from Grandma, and I think . . ."

When . . .	Say . . .
you are losing your patience with your child, instead of saying, "Why are you so annoying?"	"I am losing my patience with you!"
you are invited to an event or activity that you (or your child) would hate, instead of saying, "Traveling with your family sounds like a recipe for disaster."	"Thank you for the invitation, but I don't think that's going to work for us this weekend/ season/lifetime."
you realize you are judging a person by appearance, instead of saying, "I couldn't believe how ugly that outfit looked."	nothing.

How to Record a Video at an Event

1. **Decide what you want to capture.** Is it about allowing your child to watch footage to improve his game or capturing the milestone of performing in front of a crowd? Keep your shots wide for group activities; zoom in on faces for special performances.

2. **Prepare your equipment.** Be sure batteries are charged and your recording media has enough available storage for the movie you plan to make.

3. **Arrive early.** Scope out a good place to set up your camera. A tripod is a must-have for producing easy-on-the-eyes video clips; otherwise, you're sure to have wobbly scenes that will make your audience seasick. If the event will last longer than a few minutes, a tripod will also keep your arm from getting tired.

4. **Watch the angle.** Find a riser in the back of the room or on the sidelines that will allow your camera a view of the action that

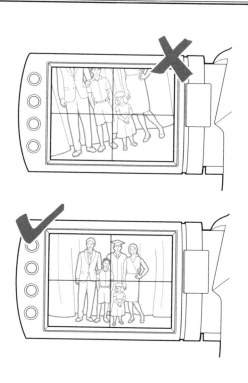

Keeping the camera parallel to the horizon line ensures a perfect shot.

excludes the backs of audience members' heads. Lock your camera into position so that any horizon—stage or landscaping—is parallel to the framing of the scene.

5. **Set it and leave it.** Constant motion can produce dizzying results; unless you have better-than-amateur videography skills, don't touch the camera while filming. To avoid mistakes during the main event, adjust focus and lighting while folks are making introductions or setting the stage.

If your child's performance is a rare special occasion and you don't want to be distracted with gadgets, ask a friend to act as cinematographer or hire a professional for the event.

Stuff You Should Know That We Can't Tell You

1. The birth dates of all your children

2. The location of the security blanket or stuffed animals that should be rescued in case of fire

3. The foods your child is allergic to

4. How much money the Tooth Fairy leaves

5. Which pizza toppings will satisfy the most members of your household

6. Your child's current shoe and clothing sizes

7. The phone number of your most reliable babysitter (and those of a few backups)

8. What your child looks like when he or she is lying

9. Which swear words are allowed in your house and at what ages

10. Which indulgence (chocolate, a long walk, trashy TV, pedicures) will be your go-to after a challenging day of parenting

Acknowledgments

We'd like to thank Julie Shpall, Ann Mary Franks, Aviva Goldfarb, Sherrie Davies, Jessica Goldman Rosenberg, Sunny McKay, Stephanie Hicks, Leslie Moss, and our readers in the RookieMoms.com community who have allowed us to deliver unsolicited advice since 2005.